SERIES EDITOR: DONALD SOMMERVILLE

OSPREY MODELLING MANUALS 20

Focke-Wulf Fw 190

RODRIGO HERNÁNDEZ CABOS AND GEOFF COUGHLIN

D1073043

OSPREY
MODELLING

First published in Great Britain in 2002 by Osprey Publishing, Elms Court,
Chapel Way, Botley, Oxford OX2 9LP United Kingdom
Email: info@ospreypublishing.com

© 2002 Osprey Publishing Ltd.
© 1992 Euro Modelismo, Accion Press, S.A., Ezequiel Solana, 16
      28017 Madrid, Spain

ISBN 1 84176 268 7

Editor: Donald Sommerville
Design: Compendium Publishing Ltd

Originated by Accion Press
Printed in China through World Print Ltd

02 03 04 05 06 10 9 8 7 6 5 4 3 2 1

**For a Catalogue of all books published by Osprey Military and Aviation
please write to:**
The Marketing Manager, Osprey Direct UK, P.O. Box 140,
Wellingborough, Northants NN8 2FA United Kingdom
Email: info@ospreydirect.co.uk

The Marketing Manager, Osprey Direct USA
c/o MBI Publishing, P.O. Box 1,
729 Prospect Ave, Osceola WI 54020, USA
Email: info@ospreydirectusa.com

www.ospreypublishing.com

Acknowledgements

The Introduction and Chapters 3 to 7 were written by Geoff
Coughlin.

Chapters 1 & 2 are by Cristobál Vergara Durán, Juan M.
Villalba Domínguez, Julio C. Cabos Gómez, Ricardo
Rodriguez Ramos and Eugenio E. Alés Ojeda.

Linework by Carlos de Diego Vaquerizo.

Colour profiles by Rodrigo Hernández Cabos.

Photographs by Carlos Salvador Gómez, Rodrigo
Hernández Cabos and Luciano Rodriguez Mosquera.

CONTENTS

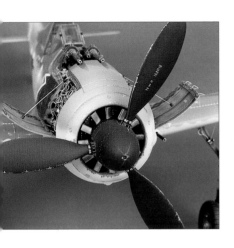

INTRODUCTION

BRIEF HISTORY OF THE Fw 190

Focke-Wulf's now infamous designer, Kurt Tank, created the Focke-Wulf 190 fighter in fact as one of a number of designs he put forward in 1937. He had to work hard to persuade the Luftwaffe that a radial engine would be as successful as the in-line engines being required in ever increasing numbers for other types of combat aircraft. The BMW 139 engine fitted to the prototype Fw 190 suffered from serious overheating problems and these continued with the first production Fw 190A-0s. The problem became so serious that the Luftwaffe considered cancelling the whole Fw 190 programme, but as we now know these early difficulties were overcome. The Fw 190 was to go on to become the mainstay of the Luftwaffe fighter force.

The first Luftwaffe unit to receive the Fw 190A-1 was JG.26 in June 1941 for operational use against the RAF along the English Channel. The RAF's first loss to an Fw 190 occurred over Dunkirk on 1 September after which it soon became clear that the German aircraft clearly had performance superior to that of the Supermarine Spitfire Mark V, the best RAF fighter of the time. There is some evidence to support the

BELOW **An early Fw 190 A-series machine. Note the small inner undercarriage doors for the main gear, deleted on later production aircraft.**

suggestion that the RAF were keen to acquire an Fw 190 in order to access its technology – even if they had to steal one!

The Fw 190 remained in service in several forms throughout the remainder of WWII, seeing considerable development of the airframe and engine. The type saw service on all fronts and as well as a day fighter, it also proved successful as a night fighter, ground-attack aircraft, long-range fighter-bomber and reconnaissance aircraft. From the outset the Fw 190 was designed to carry a wide range of machine guns, cannon, bombs, rockets, photographic equipment and even torpedoes. The aircraft could also carry additional fuel in a tank beneath the fuselage. The Fw 190, like many other aircraft from WWII received a nickname, but in this case its soubriquet of 'Butcher Bird' summed up the harsh reality of the war for its victims.

This truly successful German fighter was also designed to be very rugged, able to be maintained easily and put together by sub-contractors. All of these aims were achieved and helped its pilots achieve their outstanding combat record on the type. In fact, approximately 20,000 Fw 190s, in all versions, had been produced by the end of the war in 1945.

The Fw 190D-9 was an in-line variant of the radial-engined Fw 190, designed to improve performance above 24,000 feet, where the US bomber formations were to be found. Kurt Tank went on to submit further plans for another high-altitude fighter, the Ta 152. Development of these two high-altitude fighters took much longer to achieve and in

ABOVE **Here is an Fw 190F-8 complete with centreline and underwing bomb racks.**

5

ABOVE **An excellent close up view of an Fw 190A-4 of JG.2, probably around the time the unit was based at Vannes in France, February 1942. Note the cockerel head on the engine cowl, appearing on both sides.**

late 1943 the Luftwaffe ordered a quick solution to the problem. The Fw 190A-8/9 airframe was strengthened and lengthened to accommodate the longer Junkers Jumo 213A (bomber) engine and designated Fw 190D-9. This aircraft entered operational service in the summer of 1944. It took time for the Luftwaffe pilots to become familiar with the D-9, but they did, and the type gained more respect as performance increased. By the close of WWII, the Fw 190D-9 was able to take care of just about any Allied aircraft it came into contact with. Although about 1,500 work numbers were allocated to the type, only about 700 of these can be accounted for in confirmed production.

A number of sub-types followed on from the D-9, including the Fw 190D-11/12/13/14 and 15. These versions were only produced in very small numbers but featured some interesting colour schemes that are discussed elsewhere in this book.

The Ta 152H was a high-altitude fighter with a long wingspan, this being the most noticeable external feature at a glance to distinguish it from its earlier stable mate, the Fw 190D-9. The Ta 152 featured a Jumo 213E engine and a more widely spaced main undercarriage. The standard armament consisted of a 30mm MK108 cannon between the inverted cylinder blocks firing through the propeller hub, plus two 20mm MG151s in the inner wing roots. The first two Ta 152H development prototypes were completed in July 1944 and a test unit was formed at Rechlin with 20 Ta 152H-0 aircraft from Cottbus. Small numbers later served with JG.301, primarily providing cover during the vulnerable take-off and landing periods for the Messerschmitt 262 jet aircraft by then operating with the Luftwaffe.

HISTORY OF Fw 190 MODELLING

ABOVE **Another view of an Fw 190A-4, probably 'Yellow 11' with yellow rudder and underside of cowl.**

BELOW **The Fw 190A in 1/32 scale has been re-released by Hasegawa. Cutting Edge has also just produced an excellent resin cockpit set for the A-8 in this scale.**

The Focke-Wulf 190 was undoubtedly one of the finest fighters to operate with any air arm during WWII. Introduced in 1941 and largely taking over from the Messerschmitt Bf 109 in Luftwaffe service by the end of the war, the type changed considerably in design throughout this period. These changes have, thankfully, been reflected in the scale models that have become available over the years. All the popular scales such as 1/72, 1/48 and the larger 1/32 scale have been well served with kits of the main fighter variants of the Fw 190 like the A series.

Going back to the 1970s, many will remember the Airfix Super Kits moulded in 1/24 scale. The Spitfire, Messerschmitt Bf 109, P-51D Mustang, Hawker Hurricane and Junkers Ju 87 Stuka all received attention, and the Focke-Wulf 190 was also produced in A/F form. Several of these very good kits are currently available again, so it is just possible that Airfix will re-release this

1/48 SCALE
Focke-Wulf Fw 190 A-8/R11 NACHTJÄGER
//// TRIMASTER

ABOVE **The Trimaster Fw 190 kits were very good. Some are now available under the Revell and Italeri labels.**

very good really large-scale Fw 190, too.

Some of the most accurate, yet challenging models of the Fw 190 appeared from the Far East when Trimaster/Dragon produced their good range of models in 1/48 scale. A night fighter version, plus day fighter Fw 190A and, probably the best of the bunch, a D-9 Dora were produced. They came supplied with etched steel parts that greatly enhanced the models and were among the first kits to be produced with these accessories as standard items in the box. As has often been noted, several of the manufacturers have traded moulds over the years and this D-9 has once again appeared recently under the Italeri label. The other Trimaster/Dragon Fw 190s may well appear under the Revell label, so keep a look out for these. Revell has also produced some excellent models in 1/72 scale and the addition of the Fw 190A-8/R11 is very welcome. Until quite recently the smaller scale modeller had to rely on some pretty old offerings from the likes of Airfix, but with the turn of the century new moulds from the main manufacturers offer much more. Another case in point is a scaled down version of the excellent Tamiya Fw 190D-9 – a welcome trend from a major manufacturer that until recently has not produced a great deal in 1/72 scale.

Moving up to 1/48 or 'quarter scale', we have mentioned Tamiya, and in the 1990s this company produced two first rate models of the A-3 and F-8, the latter being the ground-attack version. Going back even further, Hasegawa produced its Fw 190A-5/8 and this featured an accurate shape but many rivets, as did the same company's Fw 190D-9. Both are now currently available again and the D-9 has come in for some helpful updating and revision – featuring a new fuselage with recessed panel lines. The Hi-Grade version also sports white metal undercarriage and propeller blades, etched fuselage items and other additions. Unfortunately, Hasegawa hasn't re-tooled the wings which are still in serious need of sanding to eliminate the excessive rivet detail and new recessed panel lines will also have to be re-scribed.

As much as the Trimaster/Dragon Fw 190s are challenging to build – mainly because of some fit problems around the fuselage/wing joints – those models produced by Tamiya in 1/48 scale are a delight to assemble. All three Fw 190s (A-3, F-8 and D-9) have very fine recessed detail and a decent level of detail on the undercarriage units and fuselage. The cockpits are fairly clean but will always be enhanced by the addition of an aftermarket accessory resin/etched detail set. Those supplied by True Details, Eduard and Verlinden are very good. Importantly, the Tamiya offerings are accurate in shape and look every bit like a scaled down version of the real aircraft. After all, that's what we modellers want, isn't it?

RADIAL-ENGINED VARIANTS

This chapter discusses four different versions of this classic fighter, all of them sub-variants of the Model A radial-engined design. The chapter begins with an A-4 in the colours used in the Tunisian campaign of early 1943 and continues with three A-8 aircraft flown by leading aces in the summer and autumn of 1944.

Throughout the next sections you will see references to various paint mixes used by the modellers concerned. Each has his own preferences. Alternatively you may prefer to use the ready-mixed RLM colours produced by manufacturers like Aeromaster, Poly-S, Testors or Hannants Xtracolour.

ABOVE **This Fw 190A-4 is seen in typical North African colours of RLM-79** *Sandgelb* **upper surfaces overall and RLM-76 under surfaces. The 'sand' upper surfaces were frequently seen mottled with olive green and the national insignia partially oversprayed with base colour.**

FOCKE-WULF 190A-4

Scale models of the Fw 190 using the colours of the North African campaign are rare but this tropical version of the fighter plane loses nothing of its appeal to the modeller.

A logical progression from the A-3 version, the Fw 190A-4 was

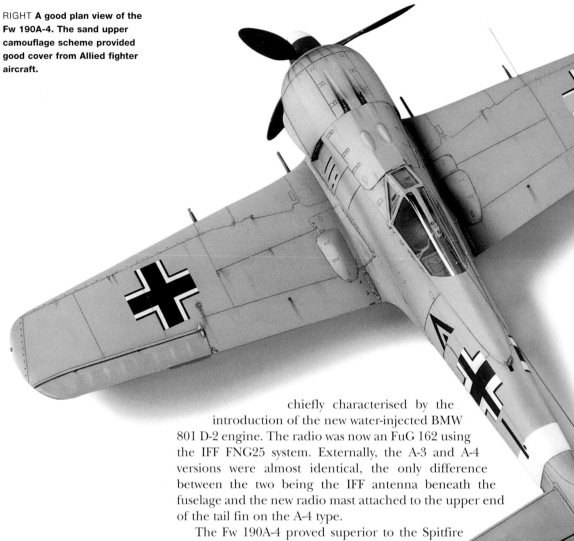

chiefly characterised by the introduction of the new water-injected BMW 801 D-2 engine. The radio was now an FuG 162 using the IFF FNG25 system. Externally, the A-3 and A-4 versions were almost identical, the only difference between the two being the IFF antenna beneath the fuselage and the new radio mast attached to the upper end of the tail fin on the A-4 type.

The Fw 190A-4 proved superior to the Spitfire Mark V and only improved fighter planes like the Spitfire Mark IX or the Hawker Typhoon could compete with it. In 1942, during engagements over the English Channel, of the 106 aircraft destroyed by the Luftwaffe, 97 were brought down by the deadly Fw 190s.

Assembly

The kit we chose as the basis for our model was the Tamiya 1/48 Fw 190A-3. The quality of this kit is excellent and the parts fit together beautifully. The decal sheet comes with insignia for four different aircraft, but these are all standard markings for planes operating on the Western Front. The kit lacks more original insignia but the large variety of decals on the market provides a solution to this problem.

We decided to convert this Fw 190A-3 into an A-4 version, and this is quite easily done. We merely needed to file down the bulky area at the top of the tail fin, replacing it with a small piece of plastic in the appropriate shape (see drawing, page 12) to form the new style of aerial.

We then started to assemble the interior of the cockpit as per the instructions. The colours for the interior are RLM-66 on the seat and floor, RLM-02 for the remainder. The paint we used is by Aeromaster. The undercarriage hatches are also in grey RLM-02, as are the fan blades immediately behind the spinner and the engine interior. Assembling the main components of the model entailed no difficulties whatsoever, and it only remained to fill the joins underneath the engine cowl with putty.

Painting

No additional improvements or etched metal parts were used in the first stage of assembly, because we intended to give maximum emphasis to the paintwork. We opted for the least familiar tropical colour scheme for the Fw 190 in North Africa, based on brown and light blue-grey. Since this is quite a simple colour combination, we needed to augment the realistic effect and appeal of the model with a range of the effects produced by long desert operations.

Once more we chose paint by Aeromaster and, after we masked off the

LEFT **The effect of small drips and oil staining can be accentuated around the engine cowl.**

LEFT **Exhaust staining was applied by airbrush to create a realistic effect. Pastel dust applied with a small brush also works well and may be easier to control.**

RIGHT **Identification markings on the fuselage.**

RIGHT **Personal insignia of the pilot, Adolf Dickfeld.**

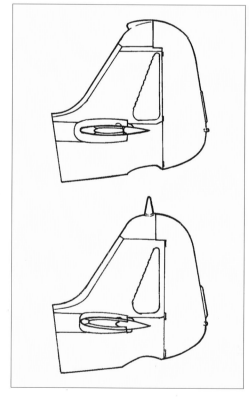

BELOW RIGHT **The more pointed aerial mast of the A-4 can clearly be seen in the lower section of this drawing – easily modified from the Tamiya A-3 kit moulded as shown above.**

BELOW **Subtle weathering on the rudder and tailplane.**

wheel wells, which we had already painted, we applied RLM-76 *Weissblau* to all the under surfaces. We then used a somewhat darker version of this same colour to produce the panel outlines. All the upper surfaces are in RLM-79 *Sandgelb* and the same procedure was repeated to produce the effect of panel outlines and structural detail. The propeller blades are in RLM-70, as is some of the propeller spinner. The front tip of the spinner is

white, darkened slightly with sand colour so that the contrast is not over-exaggerated.

To recreate the various dirt effects we used Humbrol colours. We started with a light coat of medium grey M147, and then added detail in red leather M180. If the effect seems overdone, you can cover over some of the exhaust staining with RLM-76 or RLM-79. Drips of hydraulic fluid or oil need to be done using a very fine brush and very diluted reddish black colour. These small stains can be applied to the elevators, flaps, undercarriage legs and various panels, particularly the engine cowl.

The insignia we chose belongs to the aircraft of Adolf Dickfeld, Kommandeur of II./JG.2, based at Kairouan in Tunisia at the beginning of 1943. Dickfeld eventually achieved 136 aerial victories, most of them on the Russian Front. The stripes and chevrons on the fuselage were made using black stencils (see sketch opposite). The stencils for the crosses and swastikas were airbrushed carefully using Tamiya smoke X-19, so that their white areas matched the white band on the fuselage. Tamiya smoke was again applied to exhausts, gun barrels, etc. The panel lines were accentuated using a very sharp pencil lead. Finally a coat of matt varnish finished off the model.

FOCKE-WULF 190A-8

Although currently unavailable, the 1/48 scale Dragon Fw 190A-8 kit was streets ahead of the other manufacturers' products when it was released in the 1980s. Incorporating etched steel parts and crisp although brittle plastic moulds and recessed panel lines, the model was generally considered to be very good. Many of Dragon's moulds are now appearing under the Revell or Italeri label, minus the etched parts and so there is a likelihood that the Fw 190A-8 will reappear again soon.

In this section we will build the A-8 with comparatively little modification, then later you will see how the engine compartment can be super-detailed, showing what is possible in a relatively small scale.

Assembly

Dragon is a firm that has become renowned for its quality in respect of little known aircraft, extensive decal sheets and the inclusion of photo-

RIGHT **The interior detailing was made of acetate and Plasticard.**

FAR RIGHT **The finished seat.**

BELOW RIGHT **General detail of the cockpit. The rear bulkhead was made from acetate.**

BELOW, FAR RIGHT **The fifth exhaust outlet underneath the engine cowl is missing in the kit. We made it from sheets of metal foil, flattening them slightly.**

BELOW **Guns and auxiliary cabling finished the wheel well.**

BELOW RIGHT **The positioning of the armour plating was easy.**

BOTTOM LEFT **A sheet of acetate and the metal frame comprise the armour-plated windscreen.**

BOTTOM CENTRE **Main undercarriage fully completed.**

BOTTOM RIGHT **To paint the spinner we applied a coat of white and then masked off the spiral. We then applied light green RLM-25.**

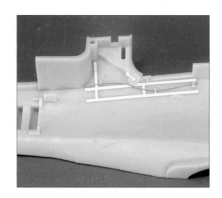
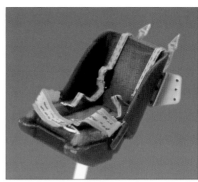
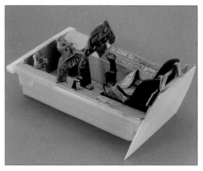

etched items in almost all of its kits. However, in this model all these qualities were undermined by the poor quality plastic and fit.

We decided to use the excellent etched metal accessory sets by Airwaves, reference AC-4826, for the armour plating, and AC-4827 for the cockpit interior, as well as the magnificent collector's reference book *Aero Detail No 6* on the Fw 190A/F.

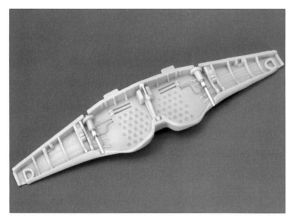

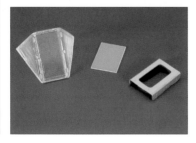

As usual, we started by working on the cockpit, clearing away poor detail and adding parts such as the control lever for the canopy, the bullet-proof visor, the flap control and electric cabling. The very accurate front instrument panel is in etched metal and includes all the necessary instruments and dials. To create the side panels, we used those provided by Airwaves, which fit perfectly. The seat is of very high quality, because it includes the seat pad and a rear armour panel. The belts provided by Dragon are very realistic, but difficult to adapt because they are hard metal, and so we decided to use those by Airwaves, cutting them down slightly in size, because they are a little wider than necessary.

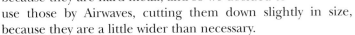

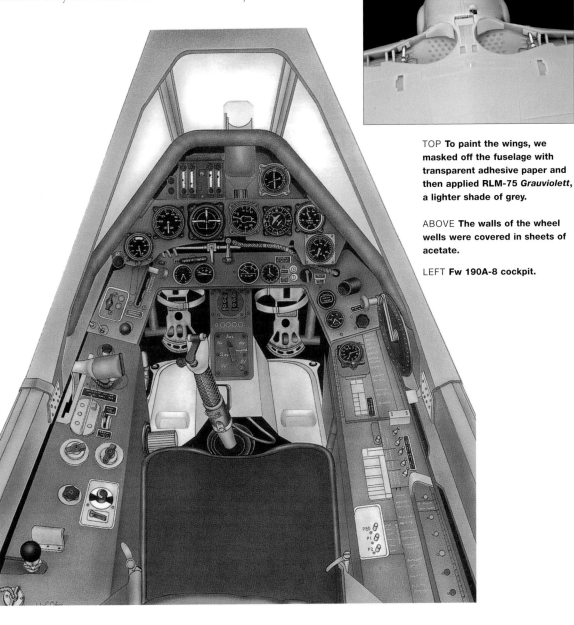

TOP **To paint the wings, we masked off the fuselage with transparent adhesive paper and then applied RLM-75 *Grauviolett*, a lighter shade of grey.**

ABOVE **The walls of the wheel wells were covered in sheets of acetate.**

LEFT **Fw 190A-8 cockpit.**

RIGHT **The mottling was done by hand, making sure that all the markings were equal in size and spaced properly.**

FAR RIGHT **To create the fuselage band we masked off a band with adhesive paper and painted it red RLM-23.**

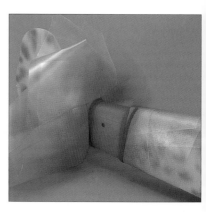

RIGHT **On the undersides of the model we reproduced the effects of wear and tear using a very dilute mixture of brown and black. The stains must not be too exaggerated.**

FAR RIGHT **The personal number of the plane is in blue, applied using adhesive masks as a template.**

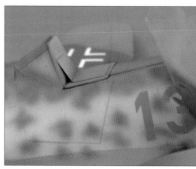

Details such as the control lever, sliding rails for the canopy and rear armour plating complete this section of the model.

The wheel wells needed some changes before assembly. The gun barrels are oversized and so we replaced these with Evergreen rods. We then added cabling made from copper wire and remodelled the sides using sheets of acetate. Once this stage was reached the model was ready to be assembled. This was not an easy task because the aperture into which the wing fits is larger than the two upper wing sections, leaving gaps in the joins which needed to be filled in with strips of Plasticard and finished off with putty. The engine cowl also fits poorly and required considerable filing down.

RIGHT **We used a paper cut-out to mask off areas when creating the weathered areas on the wings. The darker camouflage colour is RLM-74.**

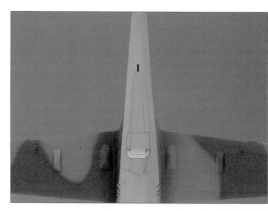

RIGHT **Although the Dragon decals are correct, we preferred to paint the crosses with an airbrush, using adhesive paper cut-outs.**

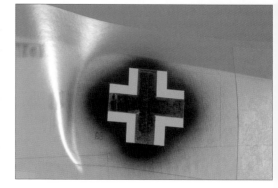

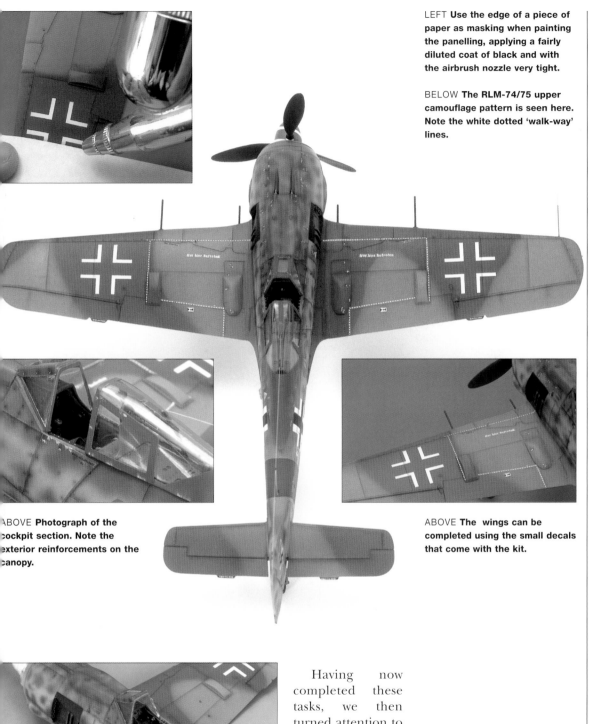

LEFT **Use the edge of a piece of paper as masking when painting the panelling, applying a fairly diluted coat of black and with the airbrush nozzle very tight.**

BELOW **The RLM-74/75 upper camouflage pattern is seen here. Note the white dotted 'walk-way' lines.**

ABOVE **Photograph of the cockpit section. Note the exterior reinforcements on the canopy.**

ABOVE **The wings can be completed using the small decals that come with the kit.**

Having now completed these tasks, we then turned attention to the undercarriage, adding the various hydraulic lines and their fastening clips, the electrical cabling to the legs, and torque links.

LEFT **The weathering effects from the exhausts were achieved using darkened sepia. Note the black paint on the panel above the airvents.**

17

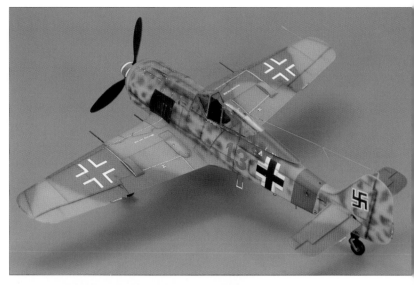

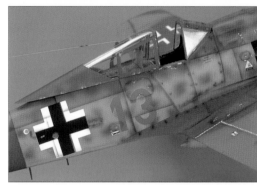

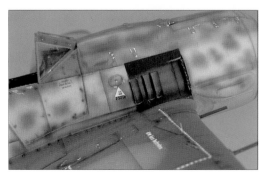

We made the hydraulic lines using PVC tubing.

The version we chose to assemble is a little unusual because it incorporates the special armour plating fitted to ground-attack aircraft. The panel by Airwaves we referred to previously is well made, and can be used for this purpose. The side plates fit perfectly, requiring only slight fingertip pressure, using cyano-acrylate glue, to attach them. Transparent areas are also all armour plated. The kit manufacturer recommends using cyano-acrylate to attach these but we avoided making this mistake because the fumes from this type of glue can damage such parts. Although white glue dries more slowly and is less adhesive it dries clear and does not do any damage. To make the windscreen we used a sheet of transparent

COLOUR CHART (ACRYLICS)

German Air Ministry Ref.	Tamiya
RLM-76 *Lichtblau*	1 pt XF-23 + 1 pt XF-19 + 3 pt XF-2
RLM-75 *Grauviolett*	12 pt XF-23 + 1 pt X-16 + 1 pt XF-24
RLM-74 *Dunkelgrau*	1 pt XF-61 + 2 pt XF-24
RLM-70 *Schwarzgrün*	1 pt XF-27 + 1 pt XF-1
RLM-23 *Rot*	XF-7
RLM-25 *Hellgrün*	1 pt XF-5 + 1 pt X-28
RLM-02 *Grau*	XF-22
RLM-41 *Grau*	XF-19

acetate for the increased thickness we needed to simulate bullet proofing.

It only remained to add small details such as the pitot tubes made out of plastic in two widths, and the guns made from hypodermic needles. We then put the aerial mast into position and the DF loop made from very very fine tin sheet. The formation lights were made from small plastic balls painted in very shiny silver and then coloured using semi-translucent acrylics by Tamiya. Stretching and heating a plastic strip and then sticking this down with cyano-acrylate can make the cable antenna. Some small touches of fairly thick paint, applied by brush, simulate the small conductors at each end of the aerial wire.

ABOVE In this photograph you can see the detailing on the mounting for the fuel tank.

Painting

To paint this Fw 190A-8 we used *The Official Monogram Painting Guide to German Aircraft 1935-45* by K.A. Merrick and T.H. Hitchcock as our main reference. This book includes photographs, colour schemes and paint samples. The particular aircraft we chose to represent is that of the ace pilot Major Walter Dahl, Kommandeur of JG.300, based at Finsterwalde

BELOW This photograph shows off to good effect the weathering and the detail added to the undercarriage legs.

COLOUR CHART (ENAMELS)			
German Air Ministry Ref.	Federal Standard	Humbrol	Xtracolor
RLM-76 *Lichtblau*	36473	HG-3	X-208
RLM-75 *Grauviolett*	36122	LG-75	X-207
RLM-74 *Dunkelgrau*	34086	HG-4	X-206
RLM-70 *Schwarzgrün*	34050	HG-1	X-204
RLM-23 *Rot*	31140	60	X-217
RLM-25 *Hellgrün*	34115		
RLM-02 *Grau*	36165	HG-6	X-409
RLM-41 *Grau*	36440		

in Germany in September 1944. In the course of his flying career Dahl achieved 129 aerial victories.

To finish a model of this kind your airbrush needs to be in tip-top condition, especially when you are trying to obtain the appropriate feathered edges for camouflage and weathering, using non-adhesive paper (to mask) or when doing the mottling patterns on the fuselage. Getting the degree of thinning of the paint and the pressure on the airbrush just right are crucially important, and it is recommended that you make trial attempts before you think of applying any colour to the model itself.

We decided to paint the crosses and the numerals using cut-outs made from masking tape, placed directly onto a drawing, instead of ready-made decals. The decal sheet supplied by Dragon is, however, very comprehensive and includes the insignia of two other famous German aces, Josef Priller and Heinz Bar.

BELOW **The completed Fw 190A-8 of Walter Dahl displayed in an airfield setting.**

The colours used in our Fw 190 correspond to the usual colour scheme of the Luftwaffe for this plane, and are as follows:

RLM-76 Light Blue
This was used to paint the underside of the wings and tail surfaces, the rudder, fuselage sides and nose, exterior components of the undercarriage and fuel tank.

RLM-75 Violet Grey
This is the brighter colour on the wings, and tail surfaces, upper surfaces of the fuselage and nose, and the leading edge of the rudder.

RLM-74 Dark Grey
Darker patches of colour on wing and tail surfaces and the upper surfaces of the fuselage and nose. It was also used to dapple the sides of the fuselage and rudder, onto the base coat of RLM-76.

RLM-70 Greenish Black
Used to paint the propeller blades.

RLM-23 Red
This was used to paint the red band on the rear section of the fuselage.

RLM-25 Light Green
Used to paint the propeller spinner in combination with a spiral of white.

RLM-02 Grey
This was used on the insides of the undercarriage doors, the main undercarriage legs and the tail wheel, the wheel wells and the front and side panels in the cockpit interior.

RLM-41 Grey
This was used for the rear section and flooring of the cockpit interior.

Fw 190A-8 JOSEF PRILLER

As we mentioned earlier in this section we have included a super-detailed model of the Dragon Fw 190A-8 kit to show what can be achieved in this quarter scale. In addition to the basic Dragon kit we have taken the Verlinden resin after market set (Ref: 438) that includes quite a lot of detail for one side of the engine. There are some problem areas and we will show you how to correct these, as well as demonstrating how to open up the wing root machine-gun bay.

Assembly
Cockpit
To construct the cockpit we used some parts from the Verlinden kit, part R-7, the lever, R-9 and the seat, R-8. We needed to take special care when putting into place the coaming for the floor, because its position is not clearly indicated.

LEFT **A coat of black paint fans out from the exhausts – this has been done using stencils and an airbrush.**

ABOVE **Note here the wavy camouflage demarcation line along the leading edge of the wing that appeared later on during WWII.**

RIGHT **Assembling the engine cowl access doors required great care and attention because they needed to be opened at the same angle.**

Pilot's Seat

We removed the moulded straps and constructed our own using tin sheeting and scratch-built copper wire buckles. We rejected both the photo-etched control panels from the kit and the Verlinden resin version and proceeded to construct new

RIGHT **The cross on each wing was painted with an airbrush. The interior of all the compartments was painted in grey RLM-02.**

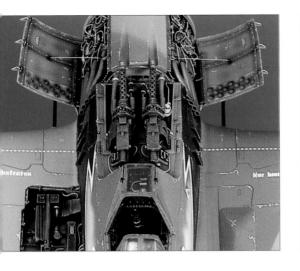

ones using plastic panels as a base and strips of acetate onto which we first drew the instruments and then covered this with transparent acetate to simulate the glass.

We painted the cockpit interior grey RLM-66, slightly darkened with an airbrush and highlighted with a dry brush to create the impression of wear and tear. We made all the additional detail, levers, cables and such, from scratch and we painted these details in acrylic colours, applied by brush. The gunsight was also built from scratch.

Armament

The Verlinden kit includes a resin part, (R-1) which can be used as a base for the 20mm MG151 wing cannon. This piece is accurate but incomplete, and we decided to rebuild all of this section, incorporating additional detail and adding all the tubes for the cooling system, the bulkhead and the upper area of the shelf at the rear of the compartment. We remodelled the brackets for the guns and added the electrical equipment and the cabling. We also made the ammunition hoppers for the guns, and included ammunition in them. We used the

ABOVE LEFT **The finest grade of Evergreen panelling was used for the perforated heat deflectors.**

ABOVE **The central section of the engine was detailed because it is visible behind the engine fan. The stencilling data on the propeller blades was reproduced using fine aluminium strips.**

BELOW **Josef Priller's Fw 190A-8 complete. Note the unusual fuselage cross.**

perforated tubes provided by the kit for the guns and reconstructed the gun barrels from hypodermic needles, achieving a conical shape by means of a mini-drill.

Engine

The Verlinden kit only provides the right hand side of the engine. The detail, although accurate, is rudimentary and we decided to reconstruct the engine entirely, adding all the detail possible.

We began by removing the original cowl that came with the kit (part C-13). We calculated the depth of the engine and made two plaques to form a support for it. To make this we stiffened two acetate sheets with longitudinal copper reinforcements, to maintain the circular shape. This support became the

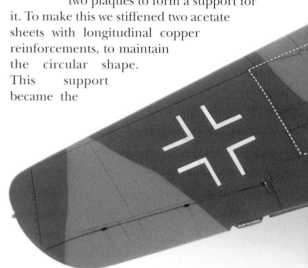

base onto which we fixed all the cylinder heads, screws, cables, etc.

The most complicated part involved the exhausts. As a base we used a round Evergreen tube, 1.5mm in diameter, filed down into an oval and then heated and bent gently to retain the original section. The heated metal staining effect was achieved with an airbrush and Tamiya acrylic paint.

This base was completed with the addition of the cowl panels, for which acetate sheets were used for the hatches and Evergreen panels for the perforated heat reflectors,

MAIN PICTURE **The overall camouflage pattern is shown here and note, too, the extensive detail within the engine compartment.**

BELOW **The small de-icing/ cleaning tubes have been put into place on the windscreen.**

TOP LEFT **Copper wire was used for all the electric cabling.**

ABOVE LEFT **All the transparent sections were polished for a more realistic effect.**

LEFT **The handles and locks of the cowl panels were made from very fine copper wire.**

ABOVE **An excellent front three-quarter view showing the unit insignia and considerable weathering.**

RIGHT **The panelling detail was reproduced using brown pencil.**

BELOW **Stencil data were added to the rudder. The antenna was made using plastic strip.**

BELOW RIGHT **The aerial wire was made in two sections – note the portion that drops down just ahead of the fin.**

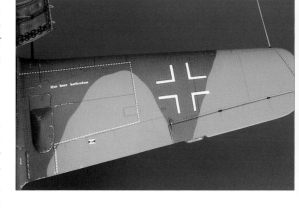

because the Verlinden kit only includes one of these parts and it is a little too large.

Gun Bay

Having assembled the photo-etched parts 6 and 7 for the box, a tricky job, we proceeded to fill in the interior using parts R-13 and R-14. We then discarded the remainder of the kit parts for this section, substituting parts which we made ourselves, such as the electric connections box, electric circuit and all the points into which the gun cover fits and which are not included in the kit.

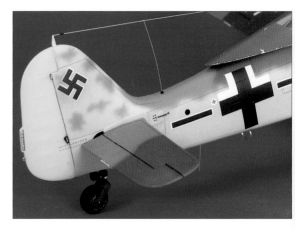

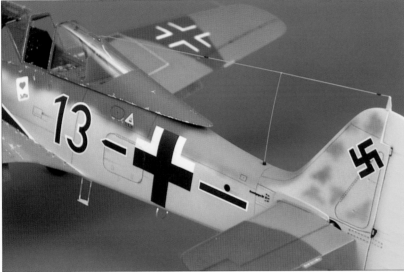

TOP LEFT **The navigation lights were reproduced using small drops of ceramic varnish.**

ABOVE **It is vital to adjust the angle of the wheels and legs correctly in this model as the characteristic 'sit' of the Fw 190 is one of its principal identification points.**

LEFT **The footrest and the antenna were scratch built.**

BELOW **The aggressive lines of the Fw 190 are evident here.**

TOP LEFT **The hydraulic line connections were made using small aluminium brackets.**

TOP RIGHT **The small light underneath the rudder compensator is totally transparent.**

ABOVE **The gun barrels were made from hypodermic needles.**

ABOVE RIGHT **The dropped flaps add a lot to the finished look and sit of the Fw 190.**

Undercarriage Bay

This is certainly the weakest point in the model because the fit is very poor, requiring total reconstruction of the sides, the structure and the gun barrels that run through the bay. It is a good idea to assemble the undercarriage doors and legs first, because they are difficult to fit if left until last.

Painting and Finishing

We opted for the personal colours of the ace Josef Priller of JG.26, as of June 1944, when he was flying an A-8 version with lighter armament which allowed for greater speed and manoeuvrability. Note that on this aircraft the cross on the fuselage does not have a white border on the lower section, that the camouflage mottling only extends onto the front portion of the fin, and that the colours on the side and fuselage are very contrasted.

The colour scheme was standard for the time, the area of operations and the aircraft. It consists of RLM-75 *Grauviolett* and RLM-74 *Dunkelgrau* on the upper surfaces and RLM-76 *Lichtblau* for the sides and undersides. The rudder and the underside of the engine cowl are yellow.

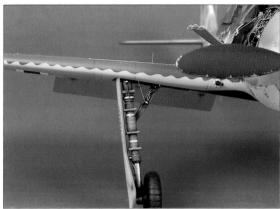

We made these shades by mixing various Tamiya colours. The combinations we used were as follows:

Hatches and gun compartments
RLM-02: 60% XF-22, 30% XF-52, 10% XF-2.

Upper section
RLM-75 *Grauviolett:* 60% XF-24, 20% XF-2 and 15% XF-7.
RLM-74 *Dunkelgrau:* 30% XF-54, 30% XF-1, 20% XF-27.

Lower Section
RLM-76 *Lichtblau:* 50% XF-19, 30% XF-23 and 15% XF-2.
    The remaining percentages to make up 100% were solvent and glue.

    All the decals were used except the crosses on the upper parts of the wings, which were painted with an airbrush. The final finish is achieved with two fine coats of Marabu satin varnish.

ABOVE LEFT **The flap is from the Verlinden kit. The interior has been reconstructed.**

ABOVE **The starboard undercarriage leg shows good detail and the wavy camouflage demarcation line on the leading edge of the wing is also evident.**

BELOW **The model is finally complete – note the excellent engine detail and the dropped flaps.**

ABOVE **Note how the completed model has the mottled fuselage pattern and spiral painted on the spinner – typical of WWII Luftwaffe fighters.**

Fw 190A-8/R-8 'RED ONE'

The Revell 1/72 scale series of Fw 190A models is something of an exception among those produced by the company. The quality of their detail and panelling and the good fit between the parts, when combined with a fairly economical price, mean these models are rare gems hidden in boxes no different from those of dozens of other Revell models which are of mediocre quality, and are often reissues of antiquated kits with quality levels which are completely outdated by today's standards.

The only significant defect in the model relates to its cockpit, as the canopy only comes moulded in the closed position, with the interior detailing attached to the windscreen. Instead of trying to carry out the difficult task of separating these parts, a simpler and more satisfactory alternative is to replace the cockpit interior with that of an Fw 190A from Hasegawa, which fits the Revell model perfectly, provided you remove any moulded-in detail first.

BELOW **The under surfaces have been very heavily weathered – but be careful not to overdo this effect.**

BELOW RIGHT **Note the areas of camouflage on the wings; in addition to using the more accurate RLM references, you have to look for a degree of contrast or feathering between the colours that is in tune with the scale of the model.**

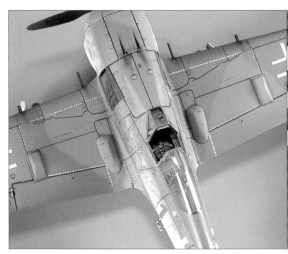

LEFT **The lighter-coloured lower surfaces constitute the ideal base upon which to reproduce the effects of wear and tear. For this model, we have combined blends of oils and pastel colours.**

Assembly

To make this specific *Ramjäger* version, we added sheets of external armour plating for the cabin, which we made from fine acetate. We also replaced the 20mm MG151 wing guns with representations of 30mm MK108 weapons, for which we had to add a few small blisters beneath the ammunition compartment panels.

In the cockpit interior we added a Revi 16B gunsight, which needed to be built onto the instrument panel; we changed the shape of the seat slightly and added on appropriate padding and attachments, which we made from bi-component putty and tin sheeting respectively. We rebuilt the headrests and shield from plastic sheeting and drilled through the little location holes that are present on each side of the instrument panel.

The base colour of the cockpit interior is a very dark grey. After this colour had been applied we added the two small parts (one transparent, the other translucent green) of which the gunsight was composed.

The exhaust pipes were made out of fine casing from electrical cable, while the guns were hypodermic needles of varying diameters, according to the calibre of the weapon they represented. A slight improvement can be achieved by replacing the wheels with those from the Hasegawa kit, while the cabling for the undercarriage was added in the form of copper wire. The wing-tip lights, made from transparent moulded plastic, look good when in place.

Painting

The markings for this model identify it as the aircraft flown by Leutnant Klaus Bretschneider, Staffelkapitän of 5./JG.300, based at Löbnitz in November 1944.

This decorative scheme of Bretschneider's aircraft was characterised by the colourful red and white spiral drawn onto the propeller spinner, which we produced using masking and an airbrush. Another distinctive feature was that the fuselage band, the number 1 and the lower part of the cowling were painted bright red, which we again completed using masking. We used a fine brush to paint the inscription *Rauhbautz VII* on the left side of the fuselage.

The colours of the camouflage, in RLM-74/75/76, were applied by airbrush, using acrylic paints, which we blended to obtain the precise shades we required. By using the base colour in different degrees of intensity, we created a panelling effect, airbrushing the darkest shade along the lines of the panels. Afterwards, we applied a coat of matt varnish to protect the work carried out and provide a good base for the next stage.

The mottle in RLM-74 and RLM-75 on the sides of the fuselage is created with a brush, using pastel chalk blended to reproduce the same colours as those of the acrylic paint. Given that pastel and acrylics react differently to varnish, we had to experiment a fair amount, using the final varnish to achieve the correct blend between the pastel colours. If you are using a brush for the varnish, it must be fine, with smooth short hairs, completely dry and clean. We also used pastels for the dirt effects on the exhaust pipes and guns.

A coat of gloss varnish then protected the pastels and prepared the surfaces for the placement of decals. We did not use the decals for the small lettering, using a brush to complete this element instead. The tail swastikas are decals. After protecting the decals with acrylic gloss varnish, we proceeded to highlight the panels on the model with oils dissolved in essence of turpentine, which we added to the lines of the panels with a brush. We also achieved the effects of dirt and oil spills using blended oil paints. The paint chipping was created using a light grey colour.

The final finish was achieved using Revell matt varnish, toned down with standard thinner. Patches of oil were touched up later with satin gloss varnish.

All the minor detail parts, painted separately, were attached following this stage so as to avoid them breaking. The final step was to attach the antenna, the correct installation of which requires it to pass through the cockpit canopy. The most durable material to make this from is fine fishing line.

This is definitely a kit that is to be highly recommended to aficionados of this aircraft. You can use it to make scale models of the Fw 190 in an infinite number of different versions and decorative schemes, as its price and quality allow you to build up an extensive collection with comparatively little effort.

RIGHT **The 'sit' of the Fw 190 is well captured here; note that the markings are weathered, too – one of the vital details in achieving a realistic finish.**

'LONG-NOSED' VARIANTS

The D-9, featured in the first part of this chapter, is probably the best-known long-nosed variant of the Fw 190 with several kits available. The interesting high-altitude variant Ta 152H is featured in the second section and is also readily available in kit form.

FOCKE-WULF 190D-9

The Fw 190D-9 is one of the World War II planes that still continues to arouse the enthusiasm of model-makers, and even more so, if this is possible, when the quality of the model attains standards of perfection such as those of the kit featured here. When we made the model shown the kit was marketed by Dragon but it was originally produced by Trimaster, albeit at an extremely high price. It is currently available from Revell at a more reasonable cost, even though it still includes etched metal parts – specifically the control panel and various antennae.

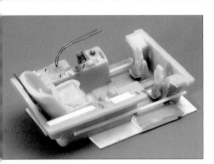

Despite its quality further improvements can be made to

LEFT **Detail of the cockpit interior with resin parts from the Verlinden accessory set for the Fw 190A-8.**

BELOW **The longer rear fuselage of the Fw 190D-9 is well illustrated here, along with the broader 'paddle-blade' propeller and extended nose section.**

ABOVE **The slightly 'stalky' appearance of the D-9 is noticeable in this view.**

RIGHT **The steel instrument panel came as an etched part in the original Dragon kit.**

FAR RIGHT **Once the decal was applied to the rear of the panel, it was painted white in the areas immediately behind the dials so that they really stand out when viewed from the front.**

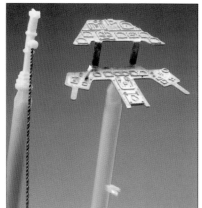

the model, the finishing touches being added in the form of elements from the Verlinden accessory set for the Fw 190A-8, from which we used selected components. The only source of documentation that we used was the book *Aero Detail No. 2: Focke-Wulf 190D*.

Assembly

Commencing assembly, as usual, with the cockpit, we added on the resin

parts: seat, levers, control column, etc.; other details, such as small cables and switches were made from fine metal wire, brass sheet and strips of plastic.

The panels were produced using the magnificent photo-etched sheet which is included with the kit and were painted

ABOVE **Revi 16B gunsight.**

ABOVE LEFT & BELOW **The interior of the cockpit is dark grey with the different colours of the controls as shown in the picture; the photo-etching is sufficiently detailed to allow it to be painted appropriately.**

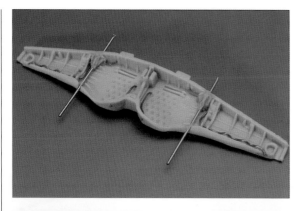

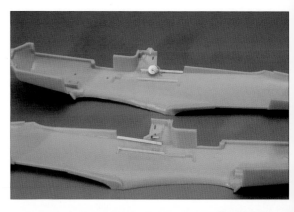

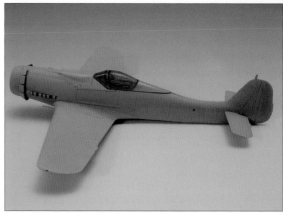

TOP LEFT **Detail in the wheel wells, with wire for hydraulic lines, hypodermic needles for gun barrels and putty for shrouding.**

TOP RIGHT **Additions to the fuselage sides using resin parts from the Verlinden accessory kit.**

ABOVE **The gun barrels were made from hypodermic needles.**

ABOVE RIGHT **First coat of paint in grey-blue, a variant upon the standard light blue.**

RIGHT **Through the openings in the wells, we can see the guns poking out and the protective mechanisms made from epoxy putty.**

according to the instructions. The general colours are a slate grey and another lighter grey.

The wells for the undercarriage are an extremely important section and their detail should be added in

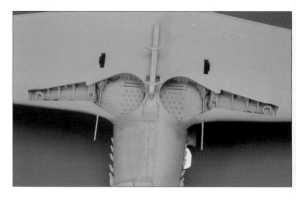

the form of fine metal wire. In addition to this the guns poke out through the wells and we made these using syringe needles with epoxy putty to create the shrouds for protection from grime and dirt.

Before closing off the fuselage, we added the control column and a few small strips of plastic on the sides.

Painting

First we protected the cabin with Maskol, sectioning off the upright struts with flexible tape. Then we applied the so-called defensive colour scheme, comprising greys and greens, more specifically:

RLM-75 Violet Grey (frontal surfaces, tail and part of the back).

RLM-83 Dark Green (mottle).

RLM-76 Light Blue (tail rudder).

RLM-24 Dark Blue (for the number 1).

RLM-71 Dark Green (nose and patches on wings).

RLM-76 Grey Blue (frontal and rear surfaces, lower and side sections of the fuselage).

The colours we used are from the Tamiya acrylic range.

The first colour used is the Grey Blue. It was a variant of RLM-76 Light Blue that was used in place of Light Blue, particularly during the closing period of the war. We created it using a mixture of XF-14 and XF-19. We covered the entire model with this colour, using it as a base colour for the rest. The rear surfaces and upper part of the

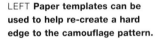

LEFT **Masking using flexible tape and Maskol.**

LEFT **Paper templates can be used to help re-create a hard edge to the camouflage pattern.**

BELOW LEFT **Each time a colour is painted on, you have to protect the other colours.**

BELOW **Low-tack transparent adhesive masking does not damage the colours.**

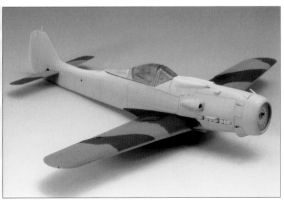

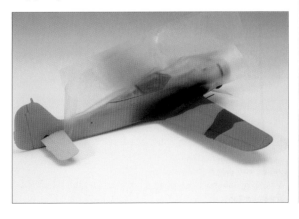

ABOVE RIGHT **The long rear
fuselage section is clearly visible
here. Again the weathering is
quite severe on this model.**

RIGHT **This camouflage of
greens and greys, known as the
'defensive scheme', produces a
striking effect.**

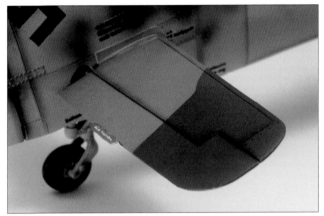

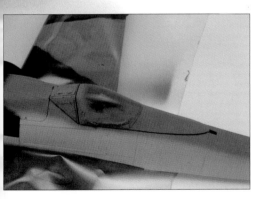

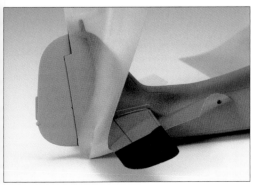

tail were then painted using RLM-75 Violet Grey. This can be obtained by mixing 80% XF-53, 10% red and 10% blue. The demarcation between the upper surface colours was made using transparent masking film while the fuselage was sprayed.

The large green camouflage sections were painted in RLM-71 Dark Green; Tamiya XF-61 is perfect and does not need to be mixed, and we used this to paint the upper surface camouflage pattern. The small and irregular mottled areas

TOP **The acrylic dries quickly and is sufficiently adhesive to allow it to be handled very soon.**

ABOVE **Multiple stencilling covers the aircraft with warnings.**

ABOVE LEFT & LEFT **Clear plastic masking film was used in several areas during finishing.**

RIGHT **The small green areas can be created by using the airbrush with your hand slightly raised.**

FAR RIGHT **The area covered by the masking must be a wide one.**

 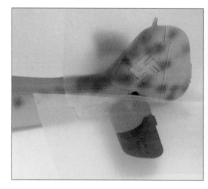

RIGHT **The underwing crosses were marked onto self adhesive film then cut out with a new scalpel blade.**

FAR RIGHT **This procedure creates nice clean edges to each cross.**

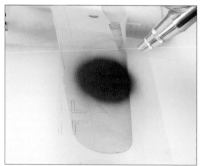 

RIGHT **Exhaust pipes were painted silver and stained with sepia inks.**

BELOW **The fuselage weathering stands out here.**

were then painted in RLM-83 Dark Green (do not be confused by the name – in reality, this was a medium shade of green). This was obtained by mixing XF-5 and XF-26; there is no need for any type of

LEFT **The clean lines of the D-9 are well shown here. Note how the aerial wire used to sag down when the canopy was opened on this version of the Fw 190.**

BELOW LEFT **Attachment of decals using a fine brush.**

BELOW **Undercarriage leg, painted here in metallic finish. RLM-02 was often used.**

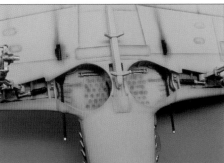

ABOVE **Precise cutting of decals.**

masking, as you carry out the painting free-hand.

To reproduce insignia that look painted on we decided to add them by spraying instead of using decals. To do this first trace them, then cut them out on an adhesive drawing mask and finally paint them using an

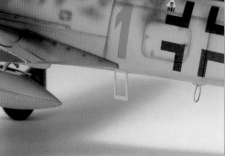

LEFT **Shading of the wells and marking of the panels, using grey inks.**

LEFT **The numbers were painted on in RLM-24 Dark Blue (Tamiya XF-23 + XF-18) using masking.**

RIGHT **Shade the panels with the help of a standard paper stencil.**

FAR RIGHT **Note the stencilling down the outer face of the undercarriage door.**

airbrush. Although this gives the best results some modellers may prefer to stick to the usual methods with decals.

The rudder brings some variety to the colour scheme, being finished in RLM-76 Light Blue. You can use Tamiya acrylic XF-23.

Use a brush to cover the exhaust pipes with silvery paint, adding sepia inks onto the silver; and then use this same shade to imitate the dirt caused by smoke, extending the coverage backwards along the fuselage above the wing, smoothly reducing the intensity as you move further back along the aircraft.

The panelling allows us to add that special touch, in the form of grey ink applied using a sheet of paper to serve as a movable mask, the colour being applied very smoothly.

RIGHT **The heavy weathering around the nose and engine compartment is clearly visible.**

BELOW **A smooth light outline was applied using sepia ink to imitate the stains around the exhaust pipe.**

BELOW RIGHT **As with the other insignia, the swastika was painted on.**

Before you go on to attach the many different decals with all the minor inscriptions, it is best to gloss varnish the whole aircraft; and, once this coat is dry, put the decals in place

ABOVE **The completed model. Note the centre-line fuel tank fitted to this Fw 190D-9.**

with the aid of a brush, varnishing again, but this time with a satin finish. Marabu varnishes are excellent and are available as sprays or in pots for use with an airbrush. Alternatively you could try those from Aeromaster, Poly-S or Revell.

FOCKE-WULF Ta 152H-1

Despite the limited involvement of this Kurt Tank design in the closing months of the so-called 'defence of the Reich', this did not obscure the outstanding qualities of a fighter that many considered to be the greatest piston-engine aircraft of the entire war.

This aircraft was designated the Ta 152 in honour of its designer, the father of all the different versions of the Fw 190, even if only this model was identified as his work in this way. The fact that it was produced so late on in the war and served with only one fighter unit, JG.301, means that there are very few photographs and little reference information about this aircraft, and even less that is of good quality. However, reliable bibliographical references exist, which we can use as our inspiration for some very attractive decorative work although, it must be admitted, they are all from the same unit and all bear the red and yellow fuselage trim of the *Reichverteidigung* to which JG.301 belonged.

The aircraft that we have modelled here was flown by Oberfeldwebel Josef 'Jupp' Keil, who finished the war with ten aerial victories, of which five were achieved with this aircraft, among them victories over a P-51 Mustang and a P-47 Thunderbolt. Keil was assigned to Stab./JG.301 based at Sachau, Germany, on 1 March 1945. To have shot down so many enemy aircraft in the short period of the war that then remained was a truly exceptional achievement, even allowing for the magnificent performance levels of this aircraft.

Not only had the Allies achieved near-overwhelming air superiority by this stage of the war, but when it entered into service, the pilots assigned to fly the Ta 152 were only allowed a single 20-minute practice flight before first taking their aircraft into combat. This was not their only problem as, due to a lack of familiarity with the silhouette of the Ta 152, they might be attacked by their comrades from other Luftwaffe units as well as by the Allied forces.

Assembly

The current Italeri model (ref. 861) is a reissue of the former Dragon version, but presented without either the photo-etched parts included by the Asian company or the parts making up the engine. This forced us to choose between two options: to assemble it as it is sold, or to acquire the resin engine parts and some etched metal accessories for the surface detail separately.

In this instance we decided to select the former option, but also to add some etched seat accessories and a certain amount of plastic to hide the enormous hole that the lack of an engine leaves in the undercarriage wheel wells.

Certain problems fitting parts together became apparent during the assembly phase, which we resolved using standard putty applied in the

ABOVE **The much longer wingspan of the Ta 152H distinguished it from the Fw 190D versions.**

TOP LEFT **This side view allows us to appreciate interesting detail. For example, the wear and tear, the smooth and controlled effect of the exhaust pipes and the minor paint chipping along the cabin opening line. Another item to highlight is that the upper half of the Balkan cross has been painted over.**

CENTRE LEFT **The fin incorporates light green mottling on top of the RLM-76 base coat.**

BOTTOM LEFT **Another characteristic of German fighters at the end of the war: the wavy border lines between the colours on the leading edge of the wing.**

normal manner. In addition to the changes already mentioned, we replaced the gun barrels on the wings and the pitot tube with tiny hollow rods (hypodermic needles or Minimeca parts). We also scratch-built the DF loop out of wire and added cabling to the landing gear and its wheel wells.

Painting and Finishing

The camouflage scheme shown in the instructions for the model, using RLM-75, is inappropriate because this was not used from mid-1944 onwards. This aircraft came into service from early 1945, and the standard scheme for Luftwaffe fighters during this later period brought together RLM-81 Brown Violet, RLM-82 Light Green and RLM-83 Dark Green, plus RLM-76 Light Blue on the lower and side surfaces of the fuselage.

Various researchers have concluded that this aircraft would have arrived at its operational unit bearing standard camouflage applied in the factory, comprising the 80-series colours mentioned above; however no one has ever given a definite ruling with regard to many aspects of

BELOW **Note the camouflage demarcation line along the fuselage and the clean lines of this high altitude type.**

WWII aircraft colours, and this is even more so for the RLMs of the Luftwaffe.

We used Tamiya and Gunze Sangyo paints exclusively. More specifically, for the darker green RLM-83 we used the Gunze H-423 shade. The light green RLM-82 is XF-5 from Tamiya and H-422 from Gunze Sangyo. For RLM-81 we applied XF-10 from Tamiya on the wings and over the Balkan cross on the fuselage, while the RLM-76 on the lower surfaces comprises a multiple-variety blend using Tamiya and Gunze colours, refs XF-23, X-2, H-47 and H-67. Alternatively you can use ready-mixed paint.

We applied all the colours in different shades, lightening or darkening them successively to achieve the realistic effect we wanted. The propeller spinner was painted using Tamiya XF-26 with the blades in matt black (at that time the familiar RLM-70 *Schwarzgrün*/Greenish Black had almost completely disappeared from use).

The cockpit interior and the undercarriage were completed in Tamiya XF-63 (RLM-66 Dark Grey), with detailing in appropriate colours. Finally, we positioned the decals having first applied a coat of gloss varnish as previously described and then gave the completed model its finishing touches with varnishes from Micro in matt and satin finish.

ABOVE **The Ta 152H had large 'paddle-shaped' propeller blades and a prominent oil cooler intake on the starboard side of the nose.**

WALKROUND

1   Champlin Fighter Aces Museum Fw 190D-13 'Yellow 10', believed to be the 17th Fw 190D-13 produced, built by Roland in March 1945. The fuselage for this D-13 was rebuilt from an old Fw 190A-8 airframe.

2   Note the open cowl flaps and large spinner of the D model.

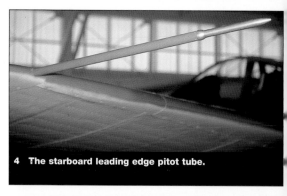

4   The starboard leading edge pitot tube.

3   The blown canopy is evident here and the 'Pik As' ('Ace of Spades') logo forward of the yellow 10.

5   Note the broad single canopy frame line running along the top of the rear sliding canopy.

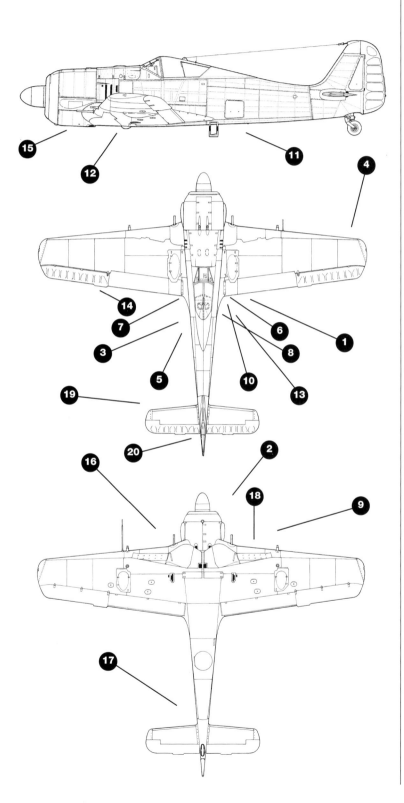

6 The Fw 109D cockpit is quite cramped, although simple in layout.

7 The port side instrument panel with throttle lever standing out.

8 The starboard side instrument panel with canopy actuator drive wheel notable.

9 Note the acute angle of the main undercarriage legs, so unique to the Fw 190 aircraft; an essential feature for the modeller to get right.

12 Useful main leg detail, note the wheel hub cap design.

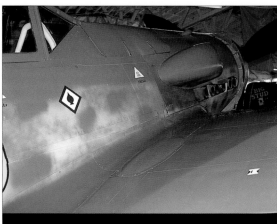

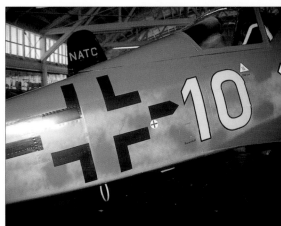

10 Note the large supercharger intake on the starboard nose, different in shape to that of the D-9.

13 You can see the smooth contours of the upper fuselage in this view.

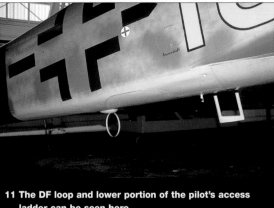

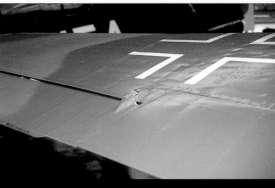

11 The DF loop and lower portion of the pilot's access ladder can be seen here.

14 The upper camouflage pattern and aileron detail on the port wing.

15 The inboard MG 151 20mm cannon.

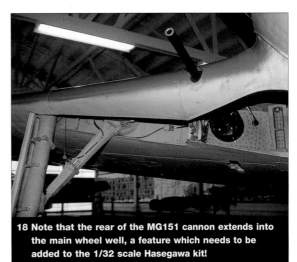

18 Note that the rear of the MG151 cannon extends into the main wheel well, a feature which needs to be added to the 1/32 scale Hasegawa kit!

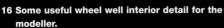

16 Some useful wheel well interior detail for the modeller.

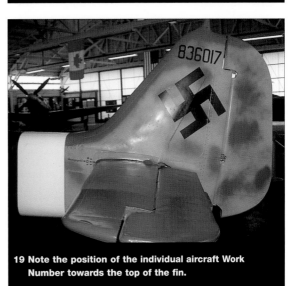

19 Note the position of the individual aircraft Work Number towards the top of the fin.

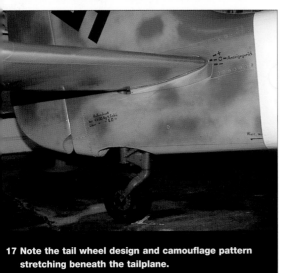

17 Note the tail wheel design and camouflage pattern stretching beneath the tailplane.

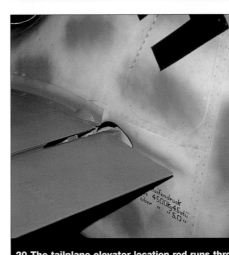

20 The tailplane elevator location rod runs through a large hole in the rear fuselage.

SCALE DRAWINGS

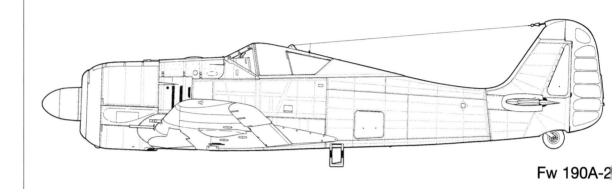

Fw 190A-2

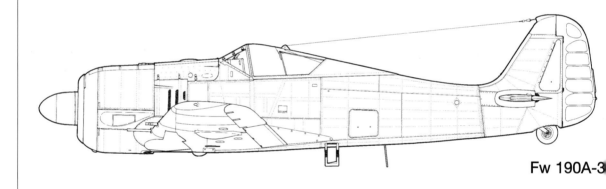

Fw 190A-3

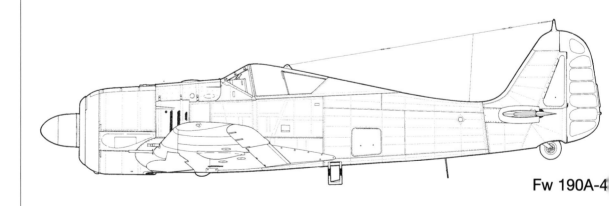

Fw 190A-4

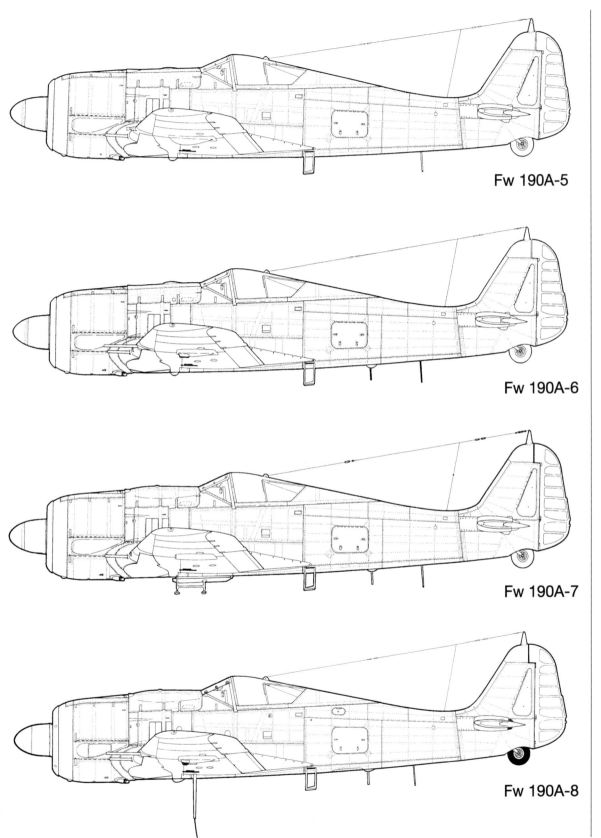

Fw 190A-5

Fw 190A-6

Fw 190A-7

Fw 190A-8

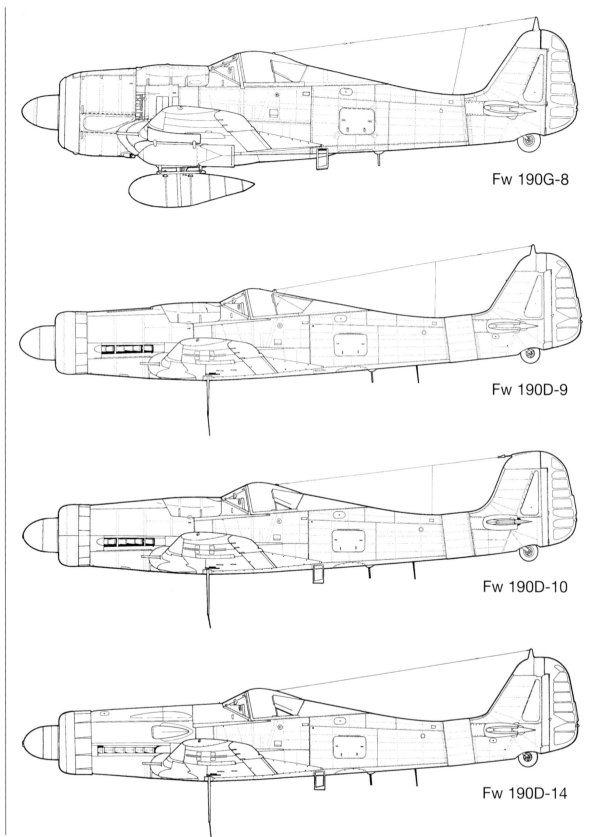

Fw 190G-8

Fw 190D-9

Fw 190D-10

Fw 190D-14

CAMOUFLAGE AND MARKINGS

The Focke-Wulf 190 featured a considerable number of camouflage and unit markings throughout its service life. In this short section we will try to identify the main schemes used on the type and draw your attention to some of the wonderful examples of 'different' patterns and markings used on some of the aircraft. In Germany, even well before WWII, the RAL organisation developed a coded system for identifying German colours and it was this that the Luftwaffe used as the basis for its schemes. In addition, the German Air Ministry, the *Reichsluftministerium*, or RLM for short, developed more colours and so the colours used acquired the prefix RLM followed by the appropriate number and name, e.g. RLM-66 *Schwarzgrau*.

The early official camouflage schemes applied to the Fw 190A series was RLM-74 *Dunkelgrau* and RLM-75 *Grauviolett* on the upper surfaces and RLM-76 *Lichtblau* covering the undersides. The fuselage sides frequently had a mottling pattern that usually looked quite soft. One or both upper surface colours were used and evidence suggests that RLM-02 was also added or used instead of one of the original colours. Of course, as you will appreciate, many units varied this approach by applying whatever colours came to hand so long as they aided camouflage from attackers.

An interesting variation that was noted on aircraft engaged in night fighter-bomber operations or Jabo raids was the application of a temporary black distemper finish. This paint was often roughly applied to the undersides and fuselage sides of the Fw 190s and wore off leaving a rather worn look on some machines.

Later in the war, the RLM issued directions for the standard 74/75/76 scheme to be changed to what are often referred to as the 'defensive colour scheme' paints of RLM-81 *Brunviolett*, 82 *Hellgrün* or 83 *Dunkelgrün* over RLM-75 undersides. The RLM-74 on the original upper surfaces was mainly altered to RLM-83. Again there were differences, with several Fw 190s featuring single upper surface colours or even RLM-70 or 71 for one or

GERMAN AIR MINISTRY COLOURS

RLM-02	*Grau*	Grey
RLM-04	*Gelb*	Yellow
RLM-21	*Weiss*	White
RLM-22	*Schwarz*	Black
RLM-23	*Rot*	Red
RLM-24	*Dunkelblau*	Dark Blue
RLM-25	*Hellgrün*	Light Green
RLM-27	*Gelb*	Yellow
RLM-41	*Grau*	Grey
RLM-65	*Hellblau*	Light Blue
RLM-66	*Schwarzgrau*	Dark Grey
RLM-70	*Schwarzgrün*	Greenish Black
RLM-71	*Dunkelgrün*	Dark Green
RLM-74	*Dunkelgrau*	Dark Grey
RLM-75	*Grauviolett*	Violet/Medium Grey
RLM-76	*Lichtblau/Weissblau*	Light Blue
RLM-77	*Hellgrau*	Light Grey
RLM-78	*Himmelblau*	Sky Blue
RLM-79	*Sandgelb*	Sand Yellow
RLM-80	*Olivgrün*	Olive Green
RLM-81	*Brunviolett*	Brown Violet
RLM-82	*Hellgrün*	Light Green
RLM-83	*Dunkelgrün*	Dark Green

RLM camouflage colours are the subject of much ongoing debate by aviation historians and modellers. There is no definitive listing, but the above list is largely based on *The Luftwaffe Modeller's Painting Guide* by Smith, Pentland and Lutz, published by Kookaburra, which is widely reckoned to be as close to definitive as is possible.

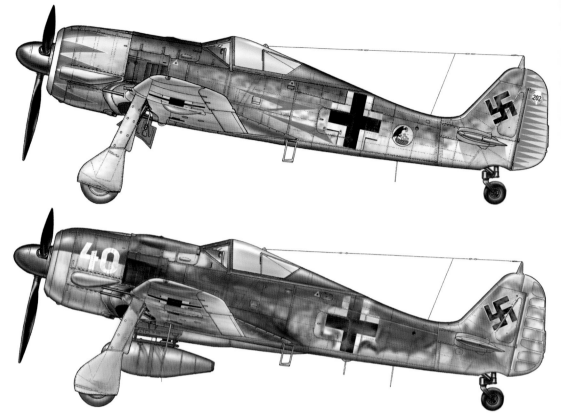

TOP **An Fw 190A-5 in the well-known markings of Major Herman Graf, France April 1943. The basic colour scheme is in RLM-74/75/76 with mottling in RLM-70/74/75/02.**

ABOVE **An Fw 190A-8 in the colours used by aircraft deployed to protect the airfields used by Me 262 jets in the last weeks of the war. The basic camouflage scheme here is in RLM-83/76/71. Unusually the under surfaces of the wings partly repeat this camouflage in RLM 83 and 76.**

both upper surface colours. It is worth noting that confusion has arisen between the correct titling for RLM-82 and 83 – the correct name for RLM-82 is *Hellgrün* and RLM-83 *Dunkelgrün*.

With attacks increasing on Luftwaffe airfields, further attempts were made to conceal their aircraft with many Fw 190s appearing in non-standard schemes – squiggles and wavy lines became common on the type. RLM-80 was often used and these markings were applied over the main camouflage scheme on the upper surfaces. Because the main landing gear was visible from above (projecting forward from below the wing) the main gear doors were also frequently over-sprayed with one of the main camouflage colours.

Among the notable features of Fw 190s are the variable and erratic colour schemes noted on several aircraft. This occurred when aircraft were sent for repair and satisfactory items salvaged from one aircraft were mated to the aircraft to be repaired. This meant that it was not uncommon to see wings in RLM-74/75/76 mated to the fuselage of another aircraft painted in 83/75/76. These variations continued throughout the war and clearly became more common towards the end of hostilities, when factories were unable to supply authorised paints in any quantities. Colours were often mixed in order to try and achieve a reasonable match or an alternative that would provide a camouflage tone.

Some texts and references refer to RLM-84, but it has to be said that no such official colour was designated by the RLM or RAL. This was a colour apparently seen on the undersides of some Fw 190s, but it is likely to have been one of the mixes we have already discussed. One variation

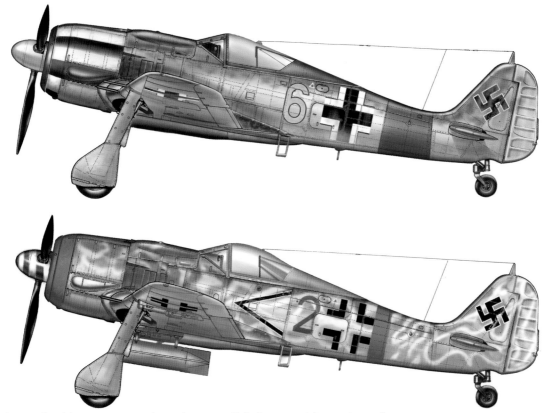

on the underside appears to have been a slightly greenish version of RLM-76.

The interior cockpit colour of the Fw 190 was RLM-66 *Schwarzgrau* applied to the instrument panel and furniture but the main interior structure of the aircraft was RLM-02. The spinner and propeller blades were officially to be mainly RLM-70, but as you can imagine, spinners often came in for repainting at unit level in many different colours, usually shaped in spirals and segments. In 1941, yellow undersides to the engine cowls appeared and yellow air to ground recognition bands appeared on Fw 190s used on the Eastern Front.

Several Luftwaffe Fw 190 units had the complete engine cowl painted with unique recognition markings, especially on those operating Fw 190As. Colourful examples were: 1./JG.1 black and white checks plus black/white spinner; 2./JG.1 red and black checks with yellow/red spinner; 3./JG.1 yellow and black checks with yellow overall spinner; and 1./JG.1, early to mid-1944 red spinner with black and white longitudinal stripes and yellow underside of the cowl.

Coloured fuselage bands were used from early on in the war to help identify friendly aircraft. Several aircraft operating on the Mediterranean Front had white fuselage bands located aft of the fuselage cross. Equally, Fw 190s operating on the Eastern Front carried yellow bands. In both cases these bands should not be confused with the *Reichverteidigung* (Reich defence) bands described below. Under-wing markings such as yellow Vs (Eastern/Western Fronts) and partial or complete painting of the underside of the main wing tips were also common. White was used for the Mediterranean theatre of operations.

TOP **An Fw 190A-7 of 3./J.61 assigned to home defence duties near Dortmund in March 1944. The camouflage scheme here is a mix of RLM-75/76/74.**

ABOVE **An Fw 190F-8/R-1 of 1./S.62, based in Hungary in January 1945. This aircraft shows the basic camouflage scheme of RLM-74/75/76 supplemented by RLM-21 White.**

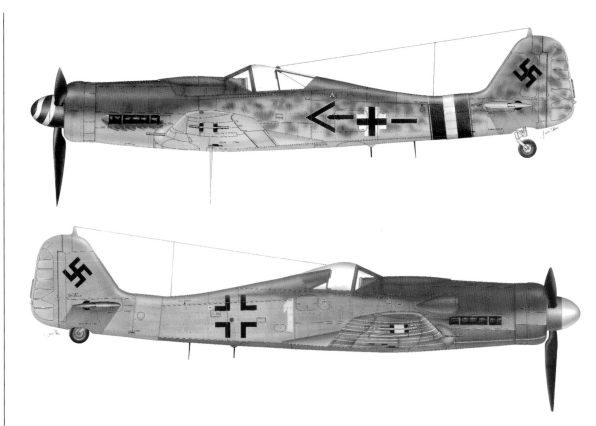

TOP **An Fw 190D-9 in a fairly standard late-war camouflage of RLM-82/83 on the upper surfaces, RLM-76 on the fuselage and underneath, and black and white spinner and insignia. This aircraft was piloted by Gerhard Miachaelski in the Frankfurt area in 1945**

ABOVE **Another Fw 190D-9 but this time in a less usual scheme with undersurfaces in RLM-23 red, with white stripes. The upper surfaces are in RLM-81 and 76. This aircraft belonged to Hauptmann Waldemar Wübke of JV.44, 1945.**

Defence of the Reich Bands

Due to Allied air superiority over Germany, an order was issued to all Jagdgeschwaderen on 20 February 1945, that all aircraft would have coloured bands painted around the fuselage ahead of the fin. The aim was to aid identification both in the air and on the ground. The bands were to have a total width of 90cm, consisting of two bands of 45cm each where two colours were used, and three bands of 30cm each when three colours were used. Despite the orders given, many aircraft appear to not have received the markings. However, Karl Ries, an acknowledged expert on Luftwaffe camouflage markings, claims that in 1944 all fighters engaged in the defence of the Reich carried a single broad red band, as for JG.1 and that in 1945, this was changed to blue/white/blue as for JG.300. It is possible that this theory is correct, as very little hard evidence exists to the contrary. In recent years, however, an excellent publication has emerged for scale modellers written by Thomas A. Tullis, *Focke Wulf 190A/F/G*. This author documents the fact that on 20 February 1945, the RLM issued Order 2/45 specifying colours and colour combinations to individual RV units. Interestingly, the document did not specify official RLM colours such as RLM-04 *Gelb*, but merely gave generic paint names like yellow red. So you can see, there is still some confusion, depending on the reference source you are using.

One variation though in fuselage band colour is the 'rust red' as applied to aircraft of JG.300 and JG.301. This colour was not taken from RLM Order 2/45, but has been adequately documented on excavated crashed aircraft. Indications show that the colour was half way between the American FS 20152 and FS 301109.

MODEL ROUND-UP

KIT AVAILABILITY
This chapter describes the kits and other items that are available in the UK at the time of writing. Manufacturers and distributors, however, alter their ranges regularly, deleting some items, issuing new ones and making formerly discontinued products available once again.

Unfortunately this means that the kits used to produce the models described in the earlier chapters of this book may not be available by the time the book is published. These chapters should therefore be understood as describing general techniques, rather than giving instructions on building specific models.

Modellers who see particular kits they may need for future projects will often do best to buy them whenever they can afford to do so to ensure that they will have them available when they are needed.

The table and listings overleaf set out to provide you with an indication of what complete kits and after market items are available for Focke-Wulf 190 modellers. In recent years there has been a huge increase in the number of additional resin, brass, injection moulded and etched metal and resin accessories. A brief synopsis of what is available is given and, importantly, this shows what is currently available at the time of writing – late 2001 in the UK. It is always possible to miss something and if you are aware of available products not mentioned here, then tell other modellers who share your interests in the Fw 190. Several manufacturers have 'promised' 'new' items for 2002, but many of these have been ignored because we have been frequently let down in the past – promises do not always turn into reality.

It is not surprising that the major variants of the Fw 190 such as the 'A', 'F' and 'D' models, are well covered by the mainstream manufacturers.

ACCESSORY AND DETAILING SETS

We have listed below the main manufacturers of resin, etched metal and other conversion kits/accessories that are currently available, together with an indication of the kind of products they offer the Focke-Wulf 190 modeller. Companies such as Aires, Eduard and Czech Master, all based in the Czech Republic, produce resin and etched accessories to a very high standard indeed. In the UK, Airwaves also offers a number of interesting sets for Fw 190 modellers. In many cases the standards achieved are truly excellent. Talking to modellers it appears that some seem to be put off by these high standards, perhaps fearing that they will not be able to do these accessories justice. This is a shame because, with patience and practice, interesting and varied models can be produced which are different from the norm. One of the benefits of adding extra detail is that it increases the options for you to display your finished Fw 190.

The following conventions are used: skill level and accuracy needed:– *** = for modellers experienced in using resin/etched

BELOW **The Tamiya Fw 190D-9 is a first class kit, easy to assemble and accurate in shape.**

Complete kits by manufacturer

	Fw 190A/F	Fw 190D	Ta 152	Other Fw 190s
Academy ** G	7	7		
Airfix ** G	2 4	7		
Dragon *** A		4	7	4 (190A & Ju 88)
				4 (D-12 torpedo)
Eduard ** G	M			
Hasegawa ** A	3 7	3 7		
Italeri ** A	7	4	4	
Matchbox ** G	7			
Monogram Pro Mod ** G				4 (G-3)
MPM ** G				7 & 4 (2-seat)
				7 (V-18)
Revell/Monogram ** G	7 4		7	4 (G-8, D-11)
				7 (Torpedo)
Sword Models ** G	7			
Tamiya ** A	7 4	7 4		

Key

7=1/72 scale; 4=1/48; 3=1/32; 2=1/24; M=other scale D=discontinued

Skill Level and Accuracy Guide:

*** = For modellers experienced in using resin/etched metal   ** = Limited level of skill required

A = Accurate   G = Generally accurate

metal, ** = limited level of skill required; A = accurate, G = generally accurate.

Aires *** A This company specializes in high quality resin accessory sets, amongst the best on the market for detail. The cockpit sets and engines are superb and also offered is a range of various guns used by the Luftwaffe. A high degree of skill is required to fit the parts, but with patience the end result can be stunning. Aires sets haven't been readily available for long but their impact on the model world has been huge.

Airwaves *** G Airwaves etched accessory sets are produced by E.D. Models in the UK. Most of the sets are formed from etched brass but resin accessories are now also available. The quality of the items produced has improved over the years and now a good range of parts and accessories for Fw 190 modellers is available. Items include guns, night fighter aerials, wheels and vac-formed canopies.

Cutting Edge Modelworks *** A This is another company that produces high quality parts and the range of items for Fw 190 modellers is growing. Revi gun sights, seats, wing cannon bulges, full conversions (A-5, 6, 7 & 8) and an excellent 1/32 A-8 cockpit set are available.

Czech Master *** A These accurate resin detail sets are very detailed and several are available for the Fw 190 fan. Accessory sets are generally offered in 1/48 scale and some gems in the catalogue include: A-8/F-8 interior, A-6/7 engine compartment, A-8/F-8 Ramjäger and an A-5/6 conversion. Others are likely to be available by the time you read this section.

Eduard *** G The Eduard company also produces kits, but is best known for its huge range of etched metal parts. The range is simply vast and you can spend many a long hour perusing lists of what they have available. The Fw 190 modeller is positively spoiled for choice in all the major scales. One of the most useful additions is the etched instrument panel with acetate dials that fits behind the main panel. The effect is excellent and very realistic. Flap detail sets are available, too.

Falcon *** G These replacement canopies are vac-formed clear replacements for the kit parts. They are generally very well moulded and clear but their greatest advantage over the kit parts is their scale thickness. They are much thinner than the polystyrene kit parts and, although tricky to remove from their backing sheet, add hugely to the finished model. This is particularly the case if you want to display your model with the canopy open.

Model Design Construction *** G MDC has some parts that will interest Fw 190 modellers such as gun sights and a cockpit interior for the D-9. As yet, the range is limited (but very good quality) and it is expected that the range will grow.

One-O-Nine *** G This company produces a good range of accessories – mainly engines, drop tanks and other items for individual Fw 190 variants.

Reheat *** G Reheat probably has the top name when it comes to instrument panels, placards and dials, and the like. The range is vast and it is easier to say go and look at the full listing. The sets invariably complement the resin detail sets that you might use from other makers and are well worth investigating if you are unfamiliar with them.

Squadron Signal *** G Clear canopies. What we've said above relating to Falcon canopies is equally relevant here.

True Details *** G This company offers a good range of resin and etched metal cockpit parts for the Fw 190 modeller. The hallmark, however, is the range of weighted tyres that is available. The company seems to have established something of a niche here with very few other manufacturers offering weighted tyres. Just occasionally, the 'flats' on these tyres look a little too flat so it is always worth checking this out with your references.

Verlinden Productions *** G This long-established manufacturer provides some good sets for the Fw 190. Its main contributions are the provision of major sets to detail the available kits, notably those for A-8 versions in 1/32.

Waldron Model Products *** A Some excellent instrument/placard sets are provided for those modelling the Airfix Super Kits like the Fw 190A/F. The main additions also include seat belts, buckles, shoulder harnesses and rudder pedals.

REFERENCES

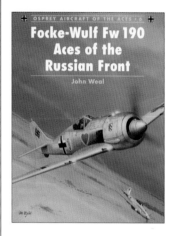

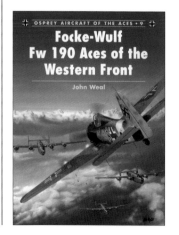

BIBLIOGRAPHY

Osprey's excellent **Aircraft of the Aces** series includes two useful titles: *Focke-Wulf Fw 190 Aces of the Russian Front*, and *Focke-Wulf Fw 190 Aces of the Western Front*, both by John Weal. This fine series is thoroughly researched. The books include good colour side profile views of different aircraft that can be used as the basis of modelling projects. By definition, the main aces' aircraft are represented: examples being Fw 190A-4 'Black Double Chevron' of Hauptmann Fritz Losigkeit, 1./JG.1, Arnhem/Deelen, Holland *circa* April–May 1943; Fw 190A-7 'Red 23' of Major Heinz Bar, Gruppenkommandeur II./JG.1 Stormede, April 1944; and finally, the very colourful Fw 190A-5 (Wk-Nr 2594) of Major Hermann Graf, Gruppenkommandeur of Jagderganzungsgruppe Ost (Operational Fighter Training Wing East), Bussac, southern France, summer 1943.

World War 2 Luftwaffe Fighter Modelling, by Geoff Coughlin, published by Osprey. This comprehensive publication contains just about everything you could want to know about modelling techniques and is aimed squarely at the Luftwaffe fighter modeller. In full colour, it breaks down all the techniques involved, as well as showing paint and colour schemes. There is a particular focus on the Fw 190 and examples of the A-4, F-8 and D-9 are all included as specific subjects.

Focke-Wulf Fw 190A/F/G, Part 1 – A Quick Reference Guide to Colours and Markings, by Thomas A. Tullis, Colortech # 1, published by Cutting Edge Modelworks. This is the first in a series of real little gems for Luftwaffe fighter modellers and includes just enough detail to be really helpful and also contains some stunning colour plates.

Luftwaffe Camouflage and Markings 1935–45 Vol 3, by J.R. Smith and J.D. Gallaspy, published Kookaburra. Well, what can you say about this volume – except that it is only one of four that are among the definitive texts dealing with Luftwaffe camouflage and markings. Explanations are exhaustive and some very good colour wartime photographs are included. The latter are quite rare and when complemented with colour side profiles, too, the result is a very useful handbook dealing with this important subject.

MUSEUMS

Very few Focke-Wulf 190s survive anywhere in the world today. There are just two original examples to be found in the UK. Otherwise the World Wide Web is an excellent starting point for trying to locate other Fw 190s that are still in existence and some useful websites are listed below which will provide you with a head start.

The examples exhibited in the UK are:–

Royal Air Force Museum, Hendon, London: Focke-Wulf 190F-8/ U1 Wk-Nr 584219. Located in the main hall, you can get good access to this aircraft for photographic purposes and to collect the detail required for modelling.

Imperial War Museum, Kennington, London: Focke-Wulf 190A-8 Wk-Nr 733682. The IWM is a veritable treasure trove for reference material and, as well as viewing the aircraft, an additional advantage of a visit here is that you can gain access to their huge bank of data and photographs (by appointment and having specified what you require).

WEBSITES AND USEFUL ADDRESSES

Hyperscale (**www.hyperscale.com**) is excellent for build articles and technical information/reviews. An information request service is available, too, through other users of the site.

The **International Plastic Modellers Society** has a wide network of branches and special interest groups throughout the world. Membership of the British section of the society also brings access to The IPMS (UK) Modelling Weekend each year plus many regional shows organised by the various local branches. A Technical Advisory service and members' Decal Bank are also features. If you require further information you should contact the Membership Administrator: Sue Allen, 8 Oakwood Close, Stenson Fields, Derby DE24 3ET; www.users.globalnet.co.uk/ ~ipmsuk.

STOCKISTS

One of the best stockists, with just about everything for the modeller is **Hannants**, Harbour Road, Oulton Broad, Lowestoft, Suffolk, NR32 3LZ, England; tel: 01502 517444; fax: 01502 500521; www.hannants.co.uk. Also well worth noting are **Historex Agents**, the UK distributor of Verlinden products, Wellington House, 157 Snargate Street, Dover, Kent, CT17 9BZ, England; tel: 01304 206720;

ABOVE & ABOVE RIGHT
Websites help suppliers give full details of their products so that you can be sure what you are getting when you buy online or by mail order. These examples show a decal set available from Hannants and a detailing kit from Verlinden.

BELOW **Many sites also feature informative kit reviews like this one from squadron.com, the site of a leading US stockist.**

fax: 01304 204528; email: sales@historex-agents.demon.co.uk. Another good stockist/mail order source is **The Aviation Hobby Shop**, 4 Horton Parade, Horton Road, West Drayton, Middlesex, UB7 8EA, England; tel: 01895 442123; fax: 01895 421412.

Hannants also stocks a wide range of accessories from many makers including the fine **AeroMaster** decals (you can also contact the company direct at www.aeromaster.com); **Eagle Editions** a specialist reference/decal supplier (also at www.eagle-editions.com), and **Cutting Edge Modelworks/Meteor Productions** for resin, etched items and decals (also at www.meteorprod.com). This company also produces the Colortech guides referred to in the bibliography. **Airwaves** brass and etched metal items can be obtained from E.D. Models, 64 Stratford Road, Shirley, Solihull, B90 3LP, England; tel: 0121 744 7488; fax: 0121 733 2591; or email: airwaves@ultramail.co.uk.

BOOKS AND MAGAZINES

A nyone who has seen *Tamiya Model Magazine International* will know about the generally high quality of production and interest in Luftwaffe projects. Highly recommended. Contact ADH Publishing, 31 High Street, Hemel Hempstead, Hertfordshire, HP1 3AA; tel: 01442 236977; fax: 01442 236988; e-mail: ModMagInt@aol.com.

Military In Scale - Model Magazine is good for reviews and specialist articles, again with good coverage of Luftwaffe types. Contact: *Military In Scale*, Traplet Publications Ltd, Traplet House, Severn Drive, Upton-Upon-Severn, Worcestershire, WR8 0JL; tel: 01684 594505; fax: 01684 594586; e-mail: mis@traplet.co.uk.

Midland Counties Publications is an excellent specialist book supplier: Unit 3, Maizefield, Hinckley, Leicestershire, LE10 1YF; tel: 01455 233747; e-mail: midlandbooks@compuserve.com.

Building an ARII Fw190A-8 into a Rammjäger | **1/48 Scale**

| Kit: AA0335 1/48th ARII FOCKE WULF Fw 190A-8
Accessories: None
Decals: Kits and Hand paint | Reference:
SS1018 Fw 190 in Action, Campbell, squadron/signal
Suggested Further References:
SS1170 Fw 190 In Action, Filly, squadron/signal
SS5522 Fw 190A/F Walk Around, Laing & Brown, squadron/signal | Paint:
Colors Gunze Paint
RLM 02 RLM Gray MAH070
RLM 66 Black Gray MAH066
RLM 74 Gray Green MAH068
RLM 75 Gray Violet MAH069
RLM 76 Light Gray MAH076
(all colors are lightened with 25% White) |